RECIPE

*Eating an artichoke
is like getting to know
someone really well.*

—Willi Hastings

COOKBOOK

PAGE

NOTES

*To invite a person into
your house is to take
charge of his happiness
for as long as he is
under your roof.*

—Brillat-Savarin

COOKBOOK

PAGE

NOTES

RECITE

A good cook is like a sorceress who dispenses happiness.

— Elsa Schiaperelli

COOKBOOK

PAGE

NOTES

RECIPE

A good meal ought to begin with hunger.

— French proverb

COOKBOOK

PAGE

NOTES

RECIPE

Life is too short to stuff a mushroom.

—Shirley Conran

COOKBOOK

PAGE

NOTES

RECIPE

I feel a recipe is only a theme which an intelligent cook can play each time with a variation.

—Madame Benoit

COOKBOOK

PAGE

NOTES

RECIPE

Too many brews spoil the cook.

—Anonymous

COOKBOOK

PAGE

NOTES

RECIPE

Don't take a butcher's advice on how to cook meat. If he knew, he'd be a chef.

—Andy Rooney

COOKBOOK

PAGE

NOTES

RECIPE

*I believe that if ever
I had to practice
cannibalism, I might
manage if there were
enough tarragon around.*

—James Beard

COOKBOOK
_____

PAGE
_____
NOTES
_____
_____
_____
_____
_____
_____
_____

RECIPE

*Garlic is the catsup
of intellectuals.*

—Anonymous

COOKBOOK
_____

PAGE
_____
NOTES
_____
_____
_____
_____
_____
_____
_____

RECITE

*I saw him even now going
the way of all flesh,
that is to say towards
the kitchen.*

—John Webster

COOKBOOK

PAGE

NOTES

RECIPE

*Probably one of the
most private things in
the world is an egg
until it is broken.*

—M. F. K. Fisher

COOKBOOK

PAGE

NOTES

RECIPE

*Eating an artichoke
is like getting to know
someone really well.*

—Willi Hastings

COOKBOOK

PAGE

NOTES

RECIPE

*To invite a person into
your house is to take
charge of his happiness
for as long as he is
under your roof.*

—Brillat-Savarin

COOKBOOK

PAGE

NOTES

RECIPE

A good cook is like a sorceress who dispenses happiness.

—Elsa Schiaperelli

COOKBOOK

PAGE

NOTES

RECIPE

A good meal ought to begin with hunger.

—French proverb

COOKBOOK

PAGE

NOTES

RECIPE

*Life is too short to
stuff a mushroom.*

—Shirley Conran

COOKBOOK

PAGE

NOTES

RECIPE

*I feel a recipe is only a
theme which an intelligent
cook can play each time
with a variation.*

—Madame Benoit

COOKBOOK

PAGE

NOTES

RECIPE

*Too many brews
spoil the cook.*

—Anonymous

COOKBOOK

PAGE

NOTES

RECIPE

*Don't take a butcher's
advice on how to
cook meat. If he knew,
he'd be a chef.*

—Andy Rooney

COOKBOOK

PAGE

NOTES

*I believe that if ever
I had to practice
cannibalism, I might
manage if there were
enough tarragon around.*

—James Beard

COOKBOOK

PAGE

NOTES

*Garlic is the catsup
of intellectuals.*

—Anonymous

COOKBOOK

PAGE

NOTES

RECISPE

*I saw him even now going
the way of all flesh,
that is to say towards
the kitchen.*

—John Webster

COOKBOOK

PAGE

NOTES

RECIPE

*Probably one of the
most private things in
the world is an egg
until it is broken.*

—M. F. K. Fisher

COOKBOOK

PAGE

NOTES

RECIPE

*Eating an artichoke
is like getting to know
someone really well.*

—Willi Hastings

COOKBOOK

PAGE

NOTES

RECIPE

*To invite a person into
your house is to take
charge of his happiness
for as long as he is
under your roof.*

—Brillat-Savarin

COOKBOOK

PAGE

NOTES

RECIPE

A good cook is like a
sorceress who dispenses
happiness.

—Elsa Schiaperelli

COOKBOOK
_____

PAGE
_____

NOTES
_____
_____
_____
_____
_____
_____
_____

RECIPE

A good meal ought to
begin with hunger.

—French proverb

COOKBOOK
_____

PAGE
_____

NOTES
_____
_____
_____
_____
_____
_____
_____

RECIPE

Life is too short to stuff a mushroom.

—Shirley Conran

COOKBOOK

PAGE

NOTES

RECIPE

I feel a recipe is only a theme which an intelligent cook can play each time with a variation.

— Madame Benoit

COOKBOOK

PAGE

NOTES